ISBN 978-0-332-73840-6
PIBN 11236362

This book is a reproduction of an important historical work. Forgotten Books uses
state-of-the-art technology to digitally reconstruct the work, preserving the original format
whilst repairing imperfections present in the aged copy. In rare cases, an imperfection in
the original, such as a blemish or missing page, may be replicated in our edition. We do,
however, repair the vast majority of imperfections successfully; any imperfections that
remain are intentionally left to preserve the state of such historical works.

TRIENNIAL AND ANNUAL

CATALOGUE,

𝕷𝖆𝖋𝖆𝖞𝖊𝖙𝖙𝖊 𝕮𝖔𝖑𝖑𝖊𝖌𝖊,

EASTON, PA.

1859.

TRIENNIAL AND ANNUAL

CATALOGUE

OF

LAFAYETTE COLLEGE,

1859.

EASTON, PA.

TRIENNIAL CATALOGUE.

BOARD OF TRUSTEES.

PRESIDENTS.

Elected.		Died or Resigned.
1826.	Hon. James M. Porter, LL.D., - -	1852.

PLEASE acknowledge the receipt of this Catalogue, that it may be known that your P. O. address is correct.

Any information you can furnish that will make the succeeding issue more correct, will be thankfully received. Direct to

PROF. WILLIAM C. CATTELL,
Clerk of Faculty.

1853. Rev. Silas M. Andrews, D.D.

BOARD OF TRUSTEES.

MEMBERS.

1826.	Gen. Robert Patterson, - - -	1835.
"	John Hare Powell, - - -	"
"	Peter A. Browne, LL.D., - - -	1849.

Please acknowledge
may be known that you. I
Any information you ca
ing issue more correct, wi

TRIENNIAL CATALOGUE.

BOARD OF TRUSTEES.

PRESIDENTS.

Elected.				Died or Resigned.
1826.	Hon. James M. Porter, LL.D.,	-	-	1852.
1852.	Rev. William McNeill, D.D.,	-	-	1853.
1853.	Rev. David McKinney, D.D.,	-	-	1857.
1857.	Rev. Septimus Tustin, D.D.			

TREASURERS.

1826.	Col. Thomas McKeen,	-	-	-	1852.
1853.	Rev. D. V. McLean, D.D.,	-	-	-	1856.
1856.	Edward J. Fox, Esq.				

SECRETARIES.

1826.	Hon. Joel Jones, L.L. D.,	-	-	1835.
1835.	Jesse M. Howell,	-	-	-	1837.
1837.	Hon. Hopewell Hepburn,	-	-	1846.
1847.	William Hackett, Esq.,	-	-	-	1853.
1853.	Rev. Silas M. Andrews, D.D.			

BOARD OF TRUSTEES.

MEMBERS.

1826.	Gen. Robert Patterson,	-	-	-	1835.
"	John Hare Powell,	-	-	-	"
".	Peter A. Browne, LL.D.,	- -	-	-	1849.

BOARD OF TRUSTEES.

BOARD OF TRUSTEES.

Elected.		Died or Resigned.
1835.	James Wilson,	1847.
"	Enoch Green,	1851.
"	Rev. Joseph McElroy, D.D.,	1849.
"	John Johnson,	1847.
1837.	Rev. Henry A. Boardman, D.D.,	1843.
"	Alexander Symington,	1848.
"	Dr. Traill Green,	1841.
"	Abraham Beidleman,	1843.
"	John J. Burke,	1852.
"	Henry Hamman,	1844.
1839.	Rev. John P. Hecht,	1845.
"	Rev. John Gray, D.D.,	1852.
1841.	Rev. John W. Yeomans,	"
"	Rev. Robert Steel, D.D.,	"
"	Rev. John Dorrance.	
1842.	Matthew L. Bevan, Esq.,	1850.
"	Rev. William R. Smith,	1847.
1843.	Hon. Charles Sitgreaves,	1853.
"	John M. Sherrerd,	1843.
"	Stacy Gardner Potts, Esq.,	1846.
"	Hon. Robert S. Kennedy,	1853.
"	Rev. Peter O. Studdiford, D.D.,	1849.
1844.	Phineas B. Kennedy, Esq.,	"
1845.	Rev. George Junkin, D.D.,	"
"	Rev. Silas M. Andrews, D.D.,	1852.
"	Richard Green,	1846.
"	William Hackett,	1853.
1846.	John Dickson,	1850.
"	Hon. William A. Porter.	
1847.	Rev. John M. Krebs, D.D.,	1853.
"	James McKeen,	1849.
"	Rev. Willis Lord, D.D.,	1852.
"	Rev. Thomas L. Janeway, D.D.,	"
"	Rev. Samuel M. Gayley,	1853.
"	Hon. Washington McCartney,	1852.

BOARD OF TRUSTEES.

6

BOARD OF TRUSTEES.

FACULTY.

—••✦••—

PRESIDENTS.

Elected.		Died or Resigned.
1832.	Rev. George Junkin, D.D., - -	1841.
1841.	" John W. Yeomans, D.D., - -	1844.
1844.	" George Junkin, D.D., - -	1848.
1849.	" Charles W. Nassau, D.D., - -	1850.
1850.	" Daniel V. McLean, D.D., - -	1857.
1857.	" George Wilson McPhail, D.D.	

VICE-PRESIDENTS.

1848.	Rev. Charles W. Nassau, - -	1849.
1849.	James H. Coffin, - - - -	1853.
1853.	Rev. George Burrowes, D.D., - -	1855.

PROFESSORS.

MENTAL AND MORAL PHILOSOPHY.

1832.	Rev. George Junkin, D.D., - -	1841.
1841.	" John W. Yeomans, D.D., -	1844.
1844.	" George Junkin, D.D., - -	1848.
1849.	Hon. Washington McCartney, -	1852.
1853.	Rev. Joseph Alden, D.D., LL.D., - -	1857.
1857.	" George Wilson McPhail, D.D.	

MATHEMATICS, NATURAL PHILOSOPHY AND ASTRONOMY.

1832.	Charles F. McCay, - - -	1833.
1834.	Samuel Galloway, - - -	1835.
1835.	Washington McCartney, - -	1836.
1837.	" " - -	1843.
1843.	William H. Green, (adjunct,) -	1844.
1844.	Washington McCartney, - -	1846.
1846.	James H. Coffin.	
1856.	Alonzo Linn, (adjunct,) - -	1857.

FACULTY.

LATIN AND GREEK LANGUAGES.

Elected.		Died or Resigned.
1832.	James J. Coon, - - - -	1837.
1836.	Alfred Ryors, (adjunct,) - -	1837.
1837.	David Moore, (adjunct,) - - -	1839.
1837.	Rev. Robert Cunningham,* - -	1839.
1839.	Samuel McCulloh, (adjunct,) - -	1840.
1839.	Clement C. Moffat, - - -	1841.
1841.	Rev. Charles W. Nassau, D.D., - -	1850.
1850.	Rev. George Burrowes, D.D., - -	1855.
1855.	Rev. William C. Cattell.	

GERMAN LANGUAGE.

1833.	Frederick Augustus Rauch, D. P. - -	1833.
1835.	Frederick Schmidt, - - -	1840.
1840.	Rev. John P. Hecht, - - -	1845.
1846.	Isidor Lowenthal, - - -	1847.
1847.	Rev. John W. Richards, - - -	1851.

CHEMISTRY.

1832.	Dr. Samuel D. Gross, - - -	1834.
1837.	Dr. Traill Green, - - -	1841.
1841.	David P. Yeomans, - - -	1845.
1845.	E. Thompson Baird, - - -	1846.
1853.	Dr. Traill Green.	

NATURAL HISTORY.

1858.	Rev. John Leaman, M. D.

MINERALOGY AND GEOLOGY.

1837.	Peter A. Browne, LL. D. - - -	1847.

BELLES LETTRES AND ENGLISH LITERATURE.

1837.	Rev. David X. Junkin, - - -	1842.
1856.	Francis A. March, (adjunct.) - -	1857.

* By appointment of the Faculty.

FACULTY.

JURISPRUDENCE AND POLITICAL ECONOMY.

Elected.   Died or Resigned.
1837. Hon. James M. Porter, LL. D. -   -   1852.

ENGLISH LANGUAGE AND PHILOLOGY.

1857. Francis A. March.

RHETORIC.

1858. Rev. James R. Eckard, D.D.

TUTORS.

1841.	William Henry Green,	-	-	-	1842.
1842.	John Lloyd,	-	-	-	-	1842.
1842.	Joseph Stevens,	-	-	-	-	1843.
1843.	Ninian Bannatyne,	-	-	-	-	1843.
1843.	Robert Newton,	-	-	-	-	1844.
1844.	Joseph Junkin,	-	-	-	-	1846.
1846.	Joseph Eastburn Nassau,	-	-	-	1848.
1848.	James T. Doran,	-	-	-	1848.
1848.	Isidor Loewenthal,	-	-	-	-	1848.
1848.	William White Cottingham,	-	-	1849.
1849.	William Francis P. Noble,	-	-	-	1850.
1851.	William White Cottingham,	-	-	1852.
1852.	Isaac G. Ogden,	-	-	-	-	1852.
1852.	Solon Albee,	-	-	-	-	1854.
1853.	Arthur Mitchell,	-	-	-	-	1854.
1854.	Alonzo Linn,	-	-	-	-	1856.
1855.	Samuel R. Gayley,	-	-	-	-	1855.
1855.	Francis A. March,	-	-	-	1856.
1857.	Alexander Scott,	-	-	-	-	1857.
1857.	Edson Ferrier,	-	-	-	-	1858.
1858.	Charles Corss.				

John Woodside, A.M.

Henry Jackson Dobbin, D.D.
    Ireland.
J. M. Junkin, A.M., *ad eundem*,
    Trenton, N. J.
Robert W. Landis, A. M.,
    New Jersey.

1847.

John Barber, A.M., Esq.
*John Brittain, A.M.
Samuel A. Gayley, A.M.
Jesse L. Howell, A.M.
Ebenezer Dickey Junkin, A.M.
Edward Kennedy, A.M.
William Kennedy, A.M., M.D.
John Fox McCoy, A.M.
Oliver Horatio Meyers, A.M., Esq.
Francis Michler, A.M., Esq.
Edmund Neff, A.M., Esq.
William Francis P. Noble, A.M.,
    Tutor.
James H. Rice, A.M.
James Wilson, A.M.

James Begg, D.D.,
    Edinburgh, Scotland.
Walter McGilvray, D.D.,
    Glasgow, Scotland.
Willis Lord, D.D., Philadelphia.
Francis C. Woodworth, A.M.,
    New York.
Samuel F. Colt, A.M., Wyalusing.
Ira B. Newman, A.M., New Jersey,
Robert K. Scott, A.M.,
    Philadelphia.

1848.

Hallock Armstrong, A.M.
William White Cottingham, A.M.,
    Tutor, T.
*Reuben Hall Crosby.
William Clark Davis, A.M.
Augustus Theodore Dobson, A.M.
James T. Doran, A.M., Tutor, T.
Alexander Fairbairn, A.M.
Spencer L. Finney, A.M.
Robert B. Foresman, A.M.
Gershom Goble, A. M.

John W. Heckman.
John Napier Husted, A.M.
Isidor Loewenthal, A.M., Tutor.
John J. A. Morgan, A.M.
James Hance Neighbour, A.M.
Garrick M. Olmstead, A.M.
John Boyd Smith, A.M.
William C. Somerville, A.M.,
    Prof. Langs., Austin Col.
Henry E. Spayd, A M.
John Squier, A.M.
Joseph P. Stidham, A.M., M.D.
Henry P. Vanderbeck,
*Jesse S. Wallace.
William Allen Wood, A.M.

John Newland, D.D.,
    Perth, Scotland.
Parsons Cook, D.D., Massachusetts.
Daniel V. McLean, D.D.,
    New Jersey.
John Johnston, D.D.,
    Newburgh, N. Y.
Lewers Dixon Gray, A.M.,
    Easton, Pa.

1849.

Samuel Holmes, A.M.
Philip W. Melick, A.M.
George W. Van Dyke, A.M., M.D.

---

*Daniel Baker, D.D., Texas.
Zebulon Butler, D.D., Mississippi.
Thomas G. Clemson, LL.D.
Robert C. Ross, A.M., Danville, Pa.
Alexander W. Rea, A.M.,
    Harrisburg, Pa.

1850.

Atcheson L. Glenn.
Abram Goodwin.
Thomas McKeen Gray, A.M.
*Traill Green, Jr.
A. Ramsay McCoy, A.M.
William Nassau, A.M., M.D.
George Taylor.

James Richards, D.D., New Jersey.

1851.

Joseph Beggs, A.M.
*Hiram A. Dietterich.
John J. Hervey Love, M.D.

John M. Dickey, D.D., Oxford, Pa.
Henry A. Longnecker, A.M.
 Allentown, Pa.
Nathaniel Michler, A.M.,
 U. S. Army.
Julius A. Fay, A.M., New Jersey.
David McCarter, A.M.,
 Strasburg, Pa.

1852.

Robert Hamill Davis, A.M.
John L. Du Bois, A.M., Esq.
David Mulford James, A.M.
Washington Scott Johnston, Esq.
Thomas L. McKeen, A.M.
James Linn McLean, A.M., Esq.
James Madison Porter, Jr., A.M.,
 Esq.
Joseph W. Porter, A.M.

Symmes C. Henry, D.D., New Jersey.
Jeremiah Sullivan Black, LL.D.,
 Pennsylvania.
George W. Porter, A.M.,
 Harrisburg, Pa.
Charles P. Bush, A.M.,
 Connecticut.
John P. Carter, A.M., Maryland.
James Scott, A.M., Attleboro', Pa.
William E. Skinner, A.B., Scotland.

1853.

Wm. Parsons Andrews, A. M., T.
Samuel R. Gayley, A.M , Tutor.
Thomas Gardner Gayley, A.M., T.
Samuel S. Kennedy, A.M., M.D.
Charles R. Mills, A.M.

Thomas Creigh, D.D,
 Mercersburg, Pa.
Lewis Cheeseman, D.D., Philadelphia.

1854.

*John B. Dorrance.
Edson Ferrier, A.M., Tutor.

Robert McCachren, A.M.
William McGalliard, T.
William Lewis Neff, Esq.

George W. Burroughs, A.M.

1855.

Hugh S. Alexander.
Robert Porter Allen, A.M., Esq.
Elisha Allis, A.M., Esq.
William M. Allison, A.M.
Charles A. Apple, A.M., T.
Robert Caldwell Bryson, A.M.
Edward L. Campbell, A.M., Esq.
William Chandler, T.
Allen Craig, A.M., Esq.
Horatio G. Fisher.
*Henry Martyn Ker.
*Thomas Miner McCarragher.
James Morgan Rawlins, A.M., T.
John Calhoun Thompson.
Henry S. Wharton, S.M.
Charles A. Wikoff, A.M., S.L.
Eugene Halsey Wood, A.M., M.D.

William Blackwood, D.D.,
 Philadelphia.
David Codwise, LL.'D.,
 New York City.

1856.

David Stuart Banks.
Richard De Charms Barclay, Esq.
Evan Miles Blanchard, S.M.
Horace Bonham.
John Clarke.
Charles Corss, Tutor.
David Kerr Freeman.
Wm. Alexander Montgomery Grier.
Lemuel Gulliver Grier, T.
Herman Hamburgher, S.L.
David Melville Heydrick.
Washington W. Hopkins, S.L.
Frank Kennedy, S.M.
Henry David T. Kerr, Esq.
*Joshua W. Ker.
Samuel Gordon Logan, S.L.
Robert M. McCormick, S.L.
Joseph Alexander Patterson.
Owen Riedy.
James McMurtrie Salmon.

Charles B. Vastine, S.M.
Joseph Paxton Vastine, Esq.

John Wier, D.D., London, Eng.
James R. Campbell, D.D., India.
Alfred Nevin, D.D., Lancaster, Pa.
James Harper, D.D.,
    Shippensburg, Pa.
Andrew Parker Porter, A.M.,
    U. S. Army.

1857.

Joseph Harrison Barnard.
John Alexander Montgomery Boyd.
Whitfield Hunt Budd, T.
John Burrows.
Enoch Clarke Cline, S.L.
David Craft, T.
Samuel Alden Freeman.
James Rich Greer, T.
Charles Hammond.
Thomas Howard, T.
Isaac Thomas Jones, S.L.
William Kennedy, S.L.
James Alexander Laughlin, T.
John Albert Liggett.
William Wilson McKinney.
Samuel Miller Moore.
John Jay Pomeroy.
Benjamin Horatio Pratt, S.M.
William Calvin Roller.
George Louis Shearer, T.
Robert Burns Snodgrass, T.
John W. Stephens, T.
Andrew Cross Trippe, S.L.
Edward Newton Vansant, S.L.
*Henry Clay Vincent.
John Calhoun Wilhelm.
Washington O. Wright.

John Leighton Wilson, D.D.,
    New York City.
Alfred Hamilton, D.D.,
    Pennsylvania.
Aaron H. Hand, D.D., New Jersey.
James E. Giffin, A.M.,
    Churchtown, Pa.
Robert F. Lehman, A.M.,
    Easton, Pa.
Samuel McLean, A.M.,
    Mauch Chunk, Pa.
William F. Lane, A.M.,
    Newcastle, Del.
Samuel Freeman, A.B.,
    Phillipsburg, N. J.

1858.

Neilson Abeel Baldwin, S.M.
William Henry Cain.
John Wesley Cline, T.
Selden Jennings Coffin, T.
Oliver Stone Dean, T.
William Hawley Dean, T.
Frank Latta DuBois, T.
Isaac X. Grier, S.L.
Edgar Wilson Hayes, T.
Charles Stewart McCormick, S.L.
Jacob Augustus Miller, S.M.
Clark Salmon.
Granville B. Slough, S.M.

Isaac V. Brown, D.D., New Jersey.
James J. Brownson, D.D.,
    Pennsylvania.
James R. Eckard, D.D.,
    Washington City.
James W. Paige, A.M.,
    Brownsville, Pa.
Charles F. Worrell, A.M.,
    New Jersey.

CATALOGUE

OF THE

OFFICERS AND MEMBERS

OF

LAFAYETTE COLLEGE,

FOR THE

YEAR 1858 9.

EASTON, PA.

TRUSTEES.

PRUDENTIAL COMMITTEE.

Rev. G. WILSON McPHAIL, D. D.
MATTHEW HALE JONES, Esq.
JAMES McKEEN, Esq.

INVESTING COMMITTEE.

JAMES McKEEN, Esq.
McEVERS FORMAN, Esq.
MATTHEW HALE JONES, Esq.

VISITORS,

APPOINTED BY THE SYNOD.

Rev. J. F. HALSEY,	Norristown, Pa.
Rev. A. B. CLARKE,	Altoona, "
Rev. J. L. VALLANDIGHAM,	Newark, Delaware.
Rev. J. H. M. KNOX,	Germantown, Phila.
Hon. GEORGE SHARSWOOD,	Philadelphia.

FACULTY.

Rev. G. WILSON McPHAIL, D. D., President,

and Professor of Mental and Moral Philosophy.

JAMES H. COFFIN, A. M.,

Professor of Mathematics and Natural Philosophy.

TRAILL GREEN, M. D.,

Professor of Chemistry.

Rev. WILLIAM C. CATTELL, A. M.

Professor of the Latin and Greek Languages.

FRANCIS A. MARCH, A. M.,

*Professor of the English Language, and Lecturer on
Comparative Philology.*

Rev. JOHN LEAMAN, A. M., M. D.,

*Professor of Natural History, and Lecturer on Human Anatomy
and Physiology.*

Rev. JAMES R. ECKARD, D. D.,

Professor of Rhetoric.

CHARLES CORSS, A. M.,

Tutor.

REFERENCES.

E. C. . . . . East College.

W. C. . . . . West College.

† . . . . Absent.

STUDENTS.

SENIORS.

NAMES.	RESIDENCES.	ROOMS.
Benjamin Gilbert Benedict,	*Patterson, N. Y.*	26 E. C.
James Penny Boyd,	*Fairfield, Lan. Co.*	25 E. C.
Joseph Castles,	*McEwensville,*	7 W. C.
H. Clay Dentler,	*McEwensville,*	60 E. C.
Joseph C. Ferriday,	*Concordia, La.*	Prof. Cattell's.
William C. Ferriday,	*Concordia, La.*	Prof. Cattell's.
John Fowler,	*Holmesburg,*	36 E. C.
T. Bradun Gillespie,	*Cecil Co., Md.*	14 E. C.
Joseph Henry Hayes,	*McEwensville,*	45 E. C.
Frank D. Hetrich,	*Easton,*	Mr. Hetrich's
Joseph Martin,	*Martin's Creek,*	7 W. C.
Henry Stothoff,	*Flemington, N. J.*	25 E. C.
Hampton Carson Watson,	*Harrisburg,*	2 W. C.
Jacob Weygandt Weaver,	*Easton,*	Mr. Weaver's.
James Raymond Weeks,	*Carmel, N. Y.*	26 E. C.
John Grier Williamson,	*York County,*	14 E. C.
John Albert Winterich,	*Oneida, N. Y.*	55 E. C.

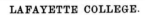

JUNIORS.

NAMES.	RESIDENCES.	ROOMS.
A. Benedict,	*Patterson, N. Y.*	21 E. C.
S. G. Blythe,	*South Hanover, Ind.*	35 E. C.
Smith P. Galt,	*Galt Villa,*	49 E. C.
J. B. Hinkson,	*Chester,*	22 E. C.
Henry T. Lee,	*Croton Falls, N. Y.*	13 E. C.
B. F. Patterson,	*Orangeville,*	27 E. C.
Jos. Patterson,	*Poundridge, N. Y.*	1 W. C.
J. B. Patton,	*Greenwood Valley,*	47 E. C.
George J. Porter,	*Chester Dist. So. Ca.*	48 E. C.
Augustus Raymond,	*Bedford, N. Y.*	3 W. C.
†S. S. Yates,	*Port Byron, N. Y.*	
R. B. Youngman,	*Mifflinburg,*	4 W. C.

SOPHOMORES.

NAMES.	RESIDENCES.	ROOMS.
Wm. H. Alexander,	*Vincennes, Ind.*	44 E. C.
A. A. Annan,	*Emmittsburg, Md.*	32 E. C.
M. N. Appleget,	*Hackettstown, N. J.*	50 E. C.
Frederic A. R. Baldwin,	*Bloomfield, N. J.*	Dr. Green's.
Joseph Barrett,	*Bedford, N. Y.*	8 W. C.
Peter S. Bergstresser,	*Berrysburg,*	23 E. C.
James K. Brugler,	*Bloomsburg,*	33 E. C.
Edward S. Carrell,	*Groveland, N. Y.*	15 E. C.
Newton James Conklin,	*Mount Morris, N. Y.*	15 E. C.
F. M. Cruikshank,	*Cecilton, Md.*	30 E C.
Luther Davis,	*Phillipsburg, N. J.*	38 E. C.
Daniel S. Dusinberre,	*Bedford, N. Y.*	1 W. C.
Samuel L. Fisler,	*Swedesboro, N. J.*	34 E. C.
Howard R. Hetrich,	*Easton,*	Mr. Hetrich's.
Thos. McCamant,	*Tipton,*	16 E. C.
†William W. Moon,	*Easton,*	
Clinton W. Neal,	*Bloomsburg,*	31 E. C.
J. M. Nourse,	*Milroy,* ——	59 E. C.
R. S. Parker,	*Lewistown,*	59 E. C.
D. I. Patterson,	*Greenwood,*	27 E C.
Jacob Person,	*Harmony, N. J.*	9 W. C.
Geo. C. Pollock,	*New York City,*	12 E. C.
Stephen W. Pomeroy,	*Roxbury,*	36 E. C.
W. H. Seip,	*Easton,*	Mr. Seip's.
W. H. Smith,	*Vincennes, Ind.*	33 E. C.
C. L. Teel,	*Phillipsburg, N. J.*	Mr L. M. Teel's.
Jacob Titman,	*Hope, N. J.*	58 E. C.
Frank B. Wells,	*Newbury, N. Y.*	34 E. C.

FRESHMEN.

NAMES.	RESIDENCES.	ROOMS.
George W. Alexander,	*Vincennes, Ind.*	44 E. C.
Frank J. Alison,	*Wilmington, Del.*	20 E. C.
John H. Buckley,	*Easton,*	Mr. Buckley's.
John Chandler,	*Belvidere, N. J.*	28 E. C.
W. H. H. Cruikshank,	*Cecilton, Md.*	30 E. C.
James Dawes,	*Easton,*	Mr. Dawes's.
Wm. Gibson Field,	*Easton,*	Dr. Field's.
H. H. Grotz,	*Bloomsburg,*	31 E. C.
Reuben Haines,	*Brick Meeting House, Md.*	8 W. C.
David A. Irwin,	*Mifflinburg,*	5 W. C.
James G. Emery,	*Flemington, N. J.*	43 E. C.
Robert I. Jones,	*Easton,*	M. H. Jones, Esq.
Brainerd Leaman,	*Easton,*	Prof. Leaman's.
Henry Page McPhail,	*Easton,*	Dr. McPhail's.
Samuel D. Mulford,	*Gloucester City, N. J.*	28 E. C.
Joseph J. Parks,	*Germantown,*	16 E. C.
Robert Scott,	*Bridesburg,*	5 W. C.
Albert N. Seip,	*Easton,*	Mr. Seip's.
Edwin Shalter,	*Schuylkill Bend,*	49 E. C.
H. W. Sherrer,	*Lewisville,*	23 E. C.
Phineas B. Vansyckel,	*Perryville, N. J.*	22 E. C.
Duncan S. Walker,	*Washington, D. C.*	56 E. C.
Henry M. Worrell,	*Perrineville, N. J.*	57 E. C.

SUMMARY.

SENIORS,	17
JUNIORS,	12
SOPHOMORES,	28
FRESHMEN,	23
TOTAL,	80

RECAPITULATION.

PENNSYLVANIA,	39
NEW YORK,	14
NEW JERSEY,	13
MARYLAND,	5
INDIANA,	4
LOUISIANA,	2
SOUTH CAROLINA,	1
DELAWARE,	1
DISTRICT OF COLUMBIA,	1

CALENDAR.

1858.

September 9, First term commences. Thursday.
Decem. 8–14, Examination of all the classes.
Decem. 15, First term ends.

Vacation of Four Weeks

1859.

January 13, Second term commences. Thursday.
April 6–12, Examination of all the classes.
April 13, Second term ends.

Vacation of Three Weeks.

May 5, Third term commences. Thursday.
June 13–15, Examination of Senior class.
July 19–25, Examination of lower classes.
July 24, Baccalaureate Sermon by the PRESIDENT, Sunday, A. M.
July 24, Sermon before the Brainerd Society by the Rev. Dr.
    PLUMER, Alleghany Theol. Seminary, Sunday, P., M.
July 25, Junior Exhibition, Monday evening.
July 26, Address before the Society of Alumni. Tuesday.
July 26, Address before the Washington and Franklin Literary
    Societies. Tuesday.
July 27, Commencement exercises. Wednesday.

Vacation of Six Weeks.

Septem. 6 and 7, Examination for admission.
Septem. 8, First term commences. Thursday.

TERMS OF ADMISSION.

CANDIDATES for admission to the Freshman class are examined in Geography, Ancient and Modern; Arithmetic; Algebra, through Simple Equations; English, Latin, and Creek Grammar, including Prosody; Cæsar's Commentaries (four books,) or Sallust; Virgil, (six books of the Æneid;) Cicero's Select Orations; Arnold's Latin Prose Composition, (xii chapters;) Xenophon's Anabasis*; the Gospels in the Greek Testament; Arnold's Greek Prose Composition, (20 §§;) or other authors fully equivalent in quantity to the above.

Candidates for advanced standing are also examined in the studies gone over by the class which they propose to enter; but no Student will be admitted to the Senior Class after the beginning of the second session.

Testimonials of good moral character are in all cases required; and those coming from other Colleges must produce certificates of dismission in good standing.

No Student is considered a regular member of College, until, after a probation of thirty days, he has been matriculated, during which time he is subject to the laws of the College.

By a resolution of the Board of Trustees every Student is required to sign a pledge that, during his College course, he will have no connection with any secret society without previous permission of the Faculty.

In the Classical Department the Grammars used are Andrews and Stoddard's Latin, and Crosby's Greek; the Lexicons, Andrews's Latin, and Liddell and Scott's Greek. Eschenburg's Manual is used as a text-book in Greek and Roman Antiquities.

* The Greek Reader will be accepted for the Anabasis.

COURSE OF INSTRUCTION.

FRESHMAN CLASS.

FIRST TERM.

Algebra, Loomis's, (commenced.)   Classical Geography.
Livy.   Old Testament, in English.
Xenophon, Cyropædia.   Lectures on Health.
Latin Composition.

SECOND TERM.

Geometry, Loomis's, (commenced.)   Greek Antiquities.
Livy.   English Composition.
Xenophon, Cyropædia   Old Testament, in English.
Latin Composition.

THIRD TERM.

Algebra, (completed.)   Greek Composition.
Geometry, (completed.)   Roman Antiquities.
Horace.   English Composition.
Herodotus.   New Testament, in English.

Throughout the Year.—Declamations, and written Translations from Greek and Latin into English.

SOPHOMORE YEAR.

FIRST TERM.

Plane Trigonometry, Loomis's.   Rhetoric.
Horace.   Greek Testament, Acts.
Xenophon, Memorabilia.   Geography of the Bible, Coleman.
Greek Composition.   Declamation, and Themes.
Study of Words, Trench.

SECOND TERM.

Conic Sections, Coffin's.   Archæology of Greek Lit. and Art.
Mensuration, Loomis's.   Greek Testament, Acts.
Homer, Iliad.   Declamation, Themes, and written
Cicero, De Oratore.   Debates.

THIRD TERM.

Navigation and Surveying, Loomis's.   Political Economy.
Homer, Iliad.   Logic.
French.   Greek Testament, Acts.
Archæology of Rom. Lit. and Art.   Declamation, Themes, and written Debates.

JUNIOR YEAR.

FIRST TERM.

Analytical Geometry, Coffin's.   German.
Differential and Integral Calculus.   History, Ancient and Modern.
Demosthenes, de Corona.   Greek Testament, Romans.
Cicero, Tusculan Disputations.   Declamation, Themes, and written Debates.

SECOND TERM.

Natural Philosophy, (commenced.)   Constitution of the United States.
Tacitus, Germania and Agricola.   Political Philosophy.
Anglo-Saxon, Barnes's Delectus.   Greek Testament, Romans.
Fowler's English Language.   Declamations, Themes, and written Debates.
Milton, Paradise Lost.

THIRD TERM.

Natural Philosophy, (continued.)   Shakespeare, Julius Cæsar.
Greek Tragedies.   Greek Testament, Ephesians.
Anglo-Saxon, Barnes's Delectus.   Declamation, Themes, and Extemporaneous Speaking.
Fowler's English Language.

SENIOR YEAR.

FIRST TERM.

Mental Philosophy, (commenced.)   Greek Literature.
Natural Philosophy, (completed.)   Rhetoric, Whately's.
Spherical Trigonometry.   Confession of Faith.
Chemistry.   Themes, and Extemporaneous Speaking.
Plato.

SECOND TERM.

Mental Philosophy, (completed.) Anatomy and Physiology.
Moral Philosophy. Juvenal and Persius.
Evidences of Christianity. Latin Literature.
Astronomy, (commenced.) English Literature.
Mineralogy. Confession of Faith.
Geology, Hitchcock's, (commenced.) Themes, and Extemporaneous
Speaking.

THIRD TERM.

Butler's Analogy. Architecture.
Astronomy, (completed.) Comparative Philology.
Geology, Hitchcock's, (completed.) Confession of Faith.
Botany. Themes, and Extemporaneous
Latin and Greek Literature, Speaking.

On Monday morning throughout the year, the Freshman, Sophomore, and Junior Classes have a Biblical Exercise, and the Seniors recite in the Confession of Faith with an Exposition.

The study of Chemistry is accompanied with a series of Lectures illustrated by experiments; that of Natural Philosophy and Astronomy, with practical illustrations and instruction in the use of instruments; that of Anatomy and Physiology, with demonstrations from Diagrams and Anatomical Specimens.

Besides the declamations in the Classes, there is a public exercise every Thursday morning in the Chapel, at which all the Classes speak by divisions, and for which they are prepared by private rehearsal before the Professor of Rhetoric. Seniors deliver Original Compositions.

Instruction is given in Hebrew gratuitously to all who desire it.

TERMS AND VACATIONS.

The College year is divided into three Terms or Sessions. The Annual Commencement is on the last Wednesday of July, and the first term of the next College year begins six weeks after, and continues fourteen weeks. A vacation of four weeks follows, after which the second term begins, and continues thirteen weeks. The last session commences on Thursday, twelve weeks preceding the Annual Commencement.

For the calendar for the present Collegiate year, see page 12.

ATTENDANCE.

Students are required to be present punctually at the commencement of each Session, and are not allowed during term time to be absent from town, except by written permission from the President or Faculty.

All the Students are required to attend Divine Service in one of the Presbyterian Churches in the borough on Sabbath Morning, (unless permitted by the Faculty to attend another Church,) and in the Chapel in the Afternoon.

A record is kept of the punctuality, diligence, scholarship, and general behaviour of each student; a report of which is sent to the parent or guardian at the close of each session.

EXAMINATIONS.

All the Classes are examined at the close of the first and second Sessions; the Senior Class is examined six weeks before Commencement; the three lower classes the week preceding Commencement, when it is the duty of a committee appointed by the Synod of Philadelphia to be present.

LOCATION.

The College is situated in the borough of Easton, Pa., fifty-five miles North from Philadelphia, and seventy-two miles West from New York. With those cities there is communication two or three times daily, (Sundays excepted,) by Railroad. Fare from $1 50 to $1 75. There

*

is also Railroad communication with the Northern Counties of Pennsylvania, and with Western New York, by means of the Belvidere Delaware, and the Delaware Lackawanna and Western Railroads; and with Central Pennsylvania, by the Lehigh Valley Railroad.

EXPENSES.

Matriculation or Admission Fee,	$3 00
Tuition per Session, (to those not on Scholarships,)	13 33
Fuel per Session, average,	2 50
Room Rent, (an average) per Session,	3 50
Servants' Wages, making Fires, &c., per Session,	1 75
For the increase of the Library, do do	68

Students are permitted to select their place of boarding, at private houses, or in clubs. The price of board in clubs is $1 25 to $2 00 per week. No student is permitted to board at a public hotel, and in all cases the place of boarding must be approved by the Faculty.

Tuition, Room Rent, and Servants' Wages must be paid each Session in advance, and no student is permitted to recite until the receipt of the Treasurer is obtained. The Matriculation or Admission Fee is paid thirty days after entering College. Students obtain washing at about one dollar per month. Students will require some money for Books and Stationery, and other incidental expenses, but it is strongly recommended to Parents to furnish them with little beyond what will meet their necessary expenses. Students provide their own furniture, fuel and lights.

LITERARY SOCIETIES.

There are two Literary Societies in the College—the Washington and the Franklin—which have spacious and well-furnished halls. Each Society has also an extensive and valuable library.

The Brainerd Evangelical Society holds its anniversary and has a public address on Sabbath Evening preceding Commencement.

On the day preceding Commencement, an oration is delivered before the Literary Societies; and one before the Society of the Alumni. The Junior Exhibition takes place on Monday evening preceding Commencement.

LIBRARY.

The College Library is open Wednesdays and Saturdays, at 9 A. M. ; that of the Franklin Society on Saturday Afternoon; of the Washington Society on Thursday Morning; and of the Brainerd Society at their regular meetings.

GRATUITOUS INSTRUCTION.

All young men of good talents who are seeking the ministry; and who are well prepared for College, will receive their tuition at a reduced rate, or gratuitously if their circumstances require it; and the Trustees design that no young man of good character and talents shall be excluded from the benefits of this Institution, on account of his inability to pay for the instruction it furnishes.

PLAN OF ENDOWMENT.

1. *One Hundred Dollars* paid shall entitle the subscriber to the tuition of all his sons, without further charge in the College;* or, instead of his own sons, those of any family he may designate; and for every additional hundred dollars which the same individual may pay, he shall have the privilege of designating the sons of any family he may think proper to receive tuition in the College as above.

2. *Five Hundred Dollars*, paid by an individual, an association of individuals, or by a congregation, shall entitle the individual, association, or session of a church or congregation to a perpetual scholarship, to which the party may appoint any individual they may select; and the scholarship may be devised by will as any other property. The incumbent on any of the scholarships is subject, of course, to all the rules and regulations of the College, as well as the discipline.

3. The Trustees bind themselves and their successors, that the funds thus contributed shall never be used for purposes inconsistent with the views of Christian truth now entertained by the Synod of Philadelphia, in connection with the General Assembly of the Presbyterian Church in the United States.

---

* The regular tuition fees for *one* student, for a full course, are ONE HUNDRED AND SIXTY DOLLARS.

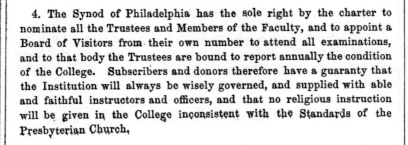

4. The Synod of Philadelphia has the sole right by the charter to nominate all the Trustees and Members of the Faculty, and to appoint a Board of Visitors from their own number to attend all examinations, and to that body the Trustees are bound to report annually the condition of the College. Subscribers and donors therefore have a guaranty that the Institution will always be wisely governed, and supplied with able and faithful instructors and officers, and that no religious instruction will be given in the College inconsistent with the Standards of the Presbyterian Church.

Lightning Source UK Ltd.
Milton Keynes UK
UKHW052035191218
334046UK00008BA/793/P